ANIMALS OF THE OCEANS
Dolphins

Judith Hodge

CONTENTS

INTRODUCTION

Dolphins are some of the most intelligent creatures on earth. They have a special relationship with people and live in nearly all the oceans.

All whales, dolphins, and porpoises are known as cetaceans. This is a group of mammals that live in the sea. They give birth to live young, which they feed with their own milk. They also breathe air at the water's surface through lungs.

Cetaceans are warm-blooded, which means that their body temperature remains relatively constant. Some animals, such as fish and lizards, are cold-blooded; their temperature changes according to the temperature of their environment.

Dolphins are toothed whales but different enough to form their own group. Species with a body length of more than nine feet are usually called whales, and species smaller than this are known as

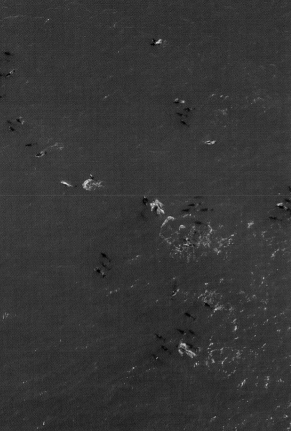

dolphins. Of course, there are a number of exceptions; the smallest whale, the dwarf sperm whale, is smaller than the largest dolphin, the bottlenose. Despite its much greater length of some thirty feet, the killer whale is also considered a dolphin.

All cetaceans have the same basic body shape. Like all toothed whales, dolphins have a blowhole in the top of their heads; rubbery, hairless skin; and a powerful fluke or tail that drives the animal through the water. Dolphins are excellent swimmers, and their streamlined shape and smooth skin reduce friction with the water.

Above: Groups of dolphins traveling together are called schools. In certain species, schools can be made up of thousands of animals.

Right: Most kinds of dolphins have a large number of teeth. They use their teeth only to grasp their prey, mainly fish and squid, which they then swallow whole.

DIFFERENT KINDS of DOLPHINS

Below: The stocky form of a Risso's dolphin is seen breaching out of the water.

There are twenty-six species that could be recognized as "classic" dolphins. They all have a distinct beak, apart from Risso's dolphin. Body shape varies from streamlined to stocky, but only two species in the group do not have a dorsal fin. None of the dolphins are over thirteen feet in length.

Many species stay near land for almost all of their lives, whereas other marine dolphins live in the open sea. Sometimes, coastal and oceanic populations of the same species can look very different. For example, coastal bottlenose dolphins are smaller than those that live in the open ocean, where they can grow up to thirteen feet long.

Dolphins are distinguished from the six species of porpoises by their well-defined, beaklike snouts, conical teeth, and different skull structure. Porpoises have a blunt snout,

4

chisel-shaped teeth, and a stouter body. None of them grow longer than eight feet.

Most species of dolphins live only in saltwater. However, there is another group that live exclusively in fresh water or the slightly salty water found in river estuaries. These primitive river dolphins are some of the smallest species, such as the four-foot susu or Indus River dolphin. They have developed a number of adaptations for life in murky rivers.

Above: Killer whales are more closely related to oceanic dolphins than to the larger whales.

Below: Porpoises are identified at sea by their smaller size and their lack of a snout.

5

BOTTLENOSE DOLPHINS

The name "bottlenose" comes from the animal's large, rounded beak, which is like the shape of an old-fashioned bottle. The color pattern varies on bottlenose dolphins, but they are typically brownish gray with a back darker than their underside. They vary in length from six to thirteen feet.

Although mostly a coastal species, bottlenose dolphins

Above: The size of coastal groups may vary according to how much food is available and the amount of protection they need against predators such as sharks.

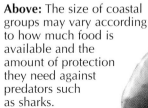

Left: Bottlenose dolphins are recognizable by their stubby beak. This makes them look like they are smiling, although the expression can't be changed.

are often seen in open waters riding the bow waves of ships. They are powerful swimmers and can reach speeds of fifteen miles an hour. The species is common in all seas from cold to tropical waters. They eat a wide variety of fish, squid, and octopuses, preferring shallow-water and bottom-dwelling species.

Bottlenose dolphins have a lifespan of over thirty years. Not surprisingly, they have a long adolescence and don't reach maturity until ten to twelve years old. A female may have up to eight calves in her lifetime.

Bottlenoses are natural acrobats, which makes them the most popular performers in sea aquariums. They have adapted well to life in captivity, and they are the best studied species of dolphin. They are also the most well known—Flipper, star of the popular television series, was a bottlenose dolphin! Whenever anyone was in trouble, Flipper would come to the rescue.

Right: Dolphins can be taught to do a wide range of tricks, such as jumping through hoops or leaping out of the water, to take fish from their trainer.

COMMON DOLPHINS

The common dolphin is one of the most abundant dolphins, as you might expect from its name. It is widespread in temperate and tropical waters, both coastal and offshore. However, in the Eastern Tropical Pacific Ocean certain local stocks are being caught in nets used for fishing tuna, greatly depleting them.

Common dolphins are one of the most colorful species with their white undersides, black backs,

Above: The common dolphin was the species most familiar to ancient Greeks and which appeared on their pottery and other artifacts. The species used to be much more common in the Mediterranean.

Right: A group of common dolphins in high-speed pursuit of a school of fish are often accompanied by seabirds that are also hunting the same prey.

Left: Yellow patches above the flipper make the common dolphin easy to identify.

and yellowish and gray-striped sides. They have perfectly streamlined and slender bodies but are usually smaller than bottlenoses, with adult sizes ranging from six to eight feet.

Common dolphins are very active and noisy. They have a wide range of whistles and sounds and can even sometimes be heard squealing as they ride on waves. Like bottlenose dolphins, they love to bow ride, not just ships but also the pressure waves generated by large whales. They are often seen breaching, slapping the water with their flippers, and doing somersaults.

Common dolphins feed on a wide variety of squid and fish, particularly schooling fish such as sardines and herring. They often work together in herds to capture food, with some of them diving below a school of fish to drive it to the surface. Here the waiting dolphins grab the fish with their teeth. With a flick of their muscular tongues, they swallow the prey whole, usually head first.

OTHER SPECIES

Most dolphins can be recognized by distinctive patterns on their bodies, particularly on the underside. In fact, of the remaining species of dolphin, a number of them are named after their appearance, such as the spotted and striped dolphins.

Spotted dolphins have long, slender bodies and pronounced beaks, similar to their close relatives, the striped and spinner dolphins. They are found in the tropical and subtropical waters of both the Atlantic and the Pacific. Spotted dolphins live in schools of fifty or more and have complex social lives. They have been kept in captivity but are not as easy to train as other species.

Occasionally bonds form between spinners and spotted dolphins, with each group taking turns to keep a lookout for sharks. Spinners hunt at night while spotted dolphins rest before taking over the "day shift."

The spinner dolphin is named after its

Left: Spinners are among the most lively and agile of all the cetaceans. Their shape and color vary greatly between groups, but they all have long, slender snouts.

Above: The amount of spotting on spotted dolphins varies both with the age and the habitat of the dolphin. The young are born without spots, which develop as they grow older, and coastal animals are more heavily spotted.

Below: The Pacific white-sided dolphin has a less-pronounced beak than most other species. Their Latin name means "slanted teeth."

habit of leaping out of the water and performing double twists and flips in the air. Spinners live in similar places to spotted dolphins and they are both very fast swimmers. Unlike spotted dolphins, spinners feed on fish and squid found in deep water.

Most of the day is spent resting close to shore, but spinner dolphins come alive in the late afternoon, leaping and splashing about. This is a sign for the rest of the animals to start moving. There is more activity as a hunting group is organized until, finally, the whole school heads out to sea.

11

Risso's dolphin, with its blunt, beakless head and stocky body, is one of the more unusual of the oceanic dolphins. Unlike the others, it feeds primarily on squid. Many of the white scars on a Risso's body are thought to have resulted from fights with squid, as well as with other adult Risso's. The animals prefer tropical and warm seas.

The dusky dolphin is found in the temperate waters of the Southern Hemisphere, off the coasts of South America, southern Africa, and New Zealand. Duskies are thought to be plentiful, but there are few surveys estimating their population. In the waters near Peru they are hunted in large numbers for their meat.

They are a relatively small species growing up to seven feet, with patches of light gray on the sides of a dark gray to blue black body. Dusky dolphins are very sociable and seem to enjoy contact

Left: Dusky dolphins are very playful, often deliberately carrying seaweed on their flippers miles out to sea in order to play games.

Left: The distinctive scarring on an adult Risso's dolphin makes it easy to identify. They also have a white belly and darker fins and flippers.

shallow-water species rarely seen more than six miles offshore. Unfortunately, this makes it vulnerable to being caught in fishing nets, although there are now a number of conservation measures to avoid this occurrance.

with people. They are often seen interacting with other species such as common and bottlenose dolphins.

Hector's dolphin grows to five feet with females being slightly longer, making it one of the smallest marine dolphins in the world. It is also one of the rarest—there are estimated to be only three to four thousand animals in the whole population.

This dolphin is found only in the coastal waters of New Zealand. It is a

Right: Hector's dolphins are easy to identify by their rounded "Mickey Mouse" dorsal fin. Their bodies are small and stocky with black, gray, and white coloring.

13

PORPOISES

All six species of porpoise (the common porpoise; Burmeister's porpoise; finless porpoise; vaquita porpoise; spectacled porpoise; and Dall's porpoise) are small, with a body length of up to seven feet and small flippers. They look quite different from dolphins as they have no beak, a rounded head, and notched tail flukes. All species, apart from the finless porpoise, have a well-defined dorsal fin.

Porpoise teeth are spade-shaped for slicing food, such as fish, too large to be eaten in one piece. This makes them unique among cetaceans. Porpoises also tend to avoid people and lack the playfulness of other species, such as bottlenose and common dolphins. They don't do well in captivity.

Above and Left: Dall's porpoise has a small tail and flippers in proportion to the rest of its body. The bulky body is made up of large muscles that enable the porpoise to swim as fast as thirty-four miles an hour.

Common porpoises, often called harbor porpoises, are the most widespread of the family. They are usually seen on their own or in small groups in the North Pacific and the cooler waters of the North Atlantic but are rarely found in tropical oceans. Common porpoises have a dark gray body that fades to a white underside.

The species feeds on small fish, such as herring and anchovies, which they find in the murky waters of bays and estuaries. Unfortunately, like Hector's dolphins, harbor porpoises frequently become trapped in fishing nets.

Dall's porpoises are found only in the cold water of the North Pacific Ocean. They are easily recognized by their black body with white patches on the sides and underneath, coloring which they share with the very rare spectacled porpoise. Dall's porpoise also has a distinctive white patch on its dorsal fin.

Above: Common porpoises swim with a slow forward roll. They don't leap out of the water like dolphins.

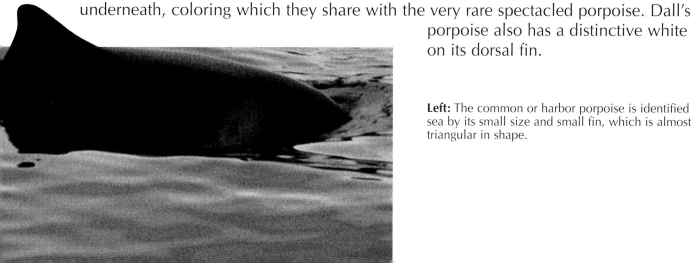

Left: The common or harbor porpoise is identified at sea by its small size and small fin, which is almost triangular in shape.

KILLER and PILOT WHALES

Despite having "whale" as part of their name, killer and pilot whales are usually grouped with dolphins. They are the largest of the dolphins but have a blunt head rather than a beak and fewer teeth. The orca or killer whale is the best known of the six species in the family that basically consists of pilot and killer whales. Little is known about the smaller species, including the pygmy killer, which is little bigger than a porpoise.

Orca are widely distributed throughout all the oceans. They are called killer whales because they feed on everything from fish and squid to marine mammals such as seals. A group will even tackle huge baleen whales much larger than themselves. People used to

Left: Orca will sometimes catch prey by coming up onto the shoreline. They grab a baby sea lion in their jaws and then turn their bodies around by vigorous use of the tail.

in the ocean, reaching speeds of up to thrity-five miles an hour.

The two species of pilot whale are distinguished from each other not only by the length of their fins but by where they live. The long-finned species is found in the colder water of the North Atlantic and Pacific Oceans, whereas the short-finned prefers tropical and temperate waters.

Above: The long-finned pilot whale has a well-defined "melon" at the front of its head, probably used in echolocation to find squid.

Below: Pygmy killer whales are closer in size to many true dolphins, but look like melon-headed whales. Despite their size, they are thought to attack other cetaceans.

be afraid of them because of their reputation as ferocious hunters, but they don't attack humans.

They are highly intelligent animals. Orca work together to herd fish or to break up or tilt ice floes on which penguins are resting.

Their distinctive black and white coloring is thought to help confuse prey by breaking up the animal's outline as it moves through the water. A killer whale's body, which can weigh up to ten tons, is almost all muscle. This is what makes it the fastest swimming mammal

RIVER DOLPHINS

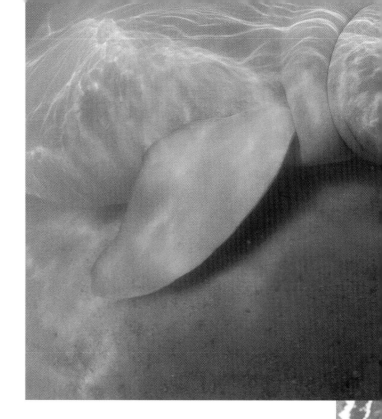

Not all dolphins live in the sea. There are five freshwater species that inhabit river estuaries in Asia and South America. They are the Amazon River dolphin; Chinese River dolphin; Ganges River dolphin; Indus River dolphin; and Franciscana, the only species that lives in both estuaries and coastal saltwater.

These river dolphins are usually grouped together, although scientists are not sure how closely they are related. It could just be that they have developed very similar features for living in murky fresh water. River dolphins are generally considered to be more primitive than oceanic dolphins.

Most of the species have tiny eyes that are virtually useless in the murky water of the rivers where they live. Some species are even completely blind. Instead of sight, river dolphins rely on echolocation to navigate and to find prey. Other features for finding their way include large flippers that they use for touch, as well as for steering and making turns in tight places.

Above: When the rivers of the Amazon burst their banks during the rainy season, the river dolphins, otherwise known as *botos* or *bufeos*, swim deep into the forest in the shallow flood water. They have been seen more than one thousand miles up the Amazon River.

Right: Many river dolphins are slow swimmers and surface regularly. They often become caught in fishing nets or are killed deliberately by fishermen who regard them as competitors for fish. Other fishers value the assistance from dolphins, which herd schools of fish into their nets.

River dolphins swim on their sides "feeling" their way as they go. Their unfused neck vertebrae allow them to move their heads separately from their bodies, unlike other dolphins. This is especially important for the *boto*, which can swim between the twisted branches and roots of trees when the Amazon River bursts its banks and floods the forest. Perhaps the most distinctive feature is the long beak with its numerous small teeth in both jaws. Some river dolphins have flattened teeth for crushing animals with shells such as crabs.

Some species are endangered. There are less than two hundred Chinese river dolphins left in the entire Yangtze River system. The Indus River species, numbering about six hundred, is also under threat from a dam that has divided the dolphins into two populations.

THE DOLPHIN'S BODY

Like their larger whale relatives, dolphins were once land-based mammals. Living in the sea meant changing over time almost every part of their body. For example, the nostrils moved to the top of the head and they developed an organ, the fatty tissue or melon, for navigation and finding prey underwater by transmitting sound waves.

One of the most obvious adaptations is the dolphin's body shape. The animals have a very streamlined body, similar to that of sharks and other large fish, which moves quickly and easily through the water. In fact, dolphins are such efficient swimmers that submarine designers have modeled new vessels on their bodies.

The skin of a dolphin is smooth for streamlining and feels like rubber. Droplets of oil released from living cells under the skin's surface further help the animal to glide through the water by

Below: Dolphins can often be seen surfing on large waves. Sometimes they bodysurf close to the beach, turning back just as the waves begin to break.

reducing friction. As in the whale's body, there is a layer of fat or blubber that keeps the animal warm. Blubber also helps the dolphin stay afloat, as fat is lighter than water.

Some dolphins have been trained to dive to more than nine hundred feet, although they don't usually dive so deeply. To do this, the animal's body adjusts to increasing water pressure by collapsing its lungs through its specially hinged ribs and decreasing its heart rate so that blood goes to the brain and heart first, before organs such as the intestine and liver.

Below: Diagram of a dolphin's body.

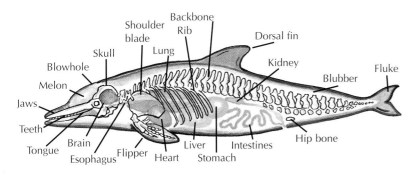

Blowhole
Melon
Jaws
Teeth
Tongue
Brain
Esophagus
Flipper
Heart
Skull
Shoulder blade
Lung
Backbone
Rib
Liver
Stomach
Intestines
Hip bone
Dorsal fin
Kidney
Blubber
Fluke

BREATHING and MOVING

A single blowhole in the top of the head identifies dolphins as toothed whales. The blowhole closes when a dolphin is underwater and opens when it comes to the surface to breathe. The animals need to breathe air at regular intervals. They must surface a couple of times every minute or so depending on how fast they are swimming.

Dolphins leap into the air as they swim along. This is so they can take a breath without slowing down. (The only porpoise to actually do this is Dall's porpoise.) Dolphins also seem to jump out of the water just for fun!

They can keep going at speeds of up to nineteen miles an hour with bursts of more than three miles an hour. However, dolphins seem to have two swimming styles—running and

Left: Strong muscles open and close the blowhole. A dolphin surfaces regularly about every two minutes to make a short explosive exhalation, followed by a longer intake of breath before going under again.

cruising. The closer they swim to the surface, the faster they are traveling and the more often they come up to take a breath.

Fins and a tail are fishlike features of dolphins, but they use them in a different way. Fish move their tails from side to side while swimming. A dolphin moves the lower part of its body, which includes the tail, in an up and down motion. This movement of the powerful tail or fluke pushes the animal forward, whereas flippers on either side of the body are used for balance.

Above and below: Leaping into the air as they swim along is an efficient way of taking a breath without reducing speed.

FEEDING and SENSES

Dolphins are faster than most of their prey, which are usually fish and squid. They can easily catch up to and seize fish with their pointed teeth. Dolphin teeth are for grasping not chewing, as food is normally swallowed whole.

Groups of dolphins have been observed "fishing" together. When they find a shoal of fish, the dolphins splash about in the water to frighten the fish and to signal to other dolphins in the area.

Dolphins can see well both above and below water. They use their eyesight to find food, to keep in contact with each other, and to watch out for predators and obstacles such as boats. They have a keen sense of touch over their entire body surface, often enjoying contact with each other and humans. Dolphins have no sense of smell and little, if any, sense of taste.

All species have a highly developed sense of hearing. They can hear a wide range of low- and high-pitched sounds, including many that can't be heard by people.

Above: Dusky dolphins often fish in groups, sometimes tail-slapping or jumping about. They use their bodies in this way to herd fish to locations where other duskies are waiting to feast on them.

24

Right: Beaching in dolphins could be due to a malfunction in their echolocation system. This may be caused by the shallow shelving of a particular part of the coast, especially in muddy estuaries, or by parasites in the animal's ears that confuse the signals.

Below: Diagram showing echolocation.

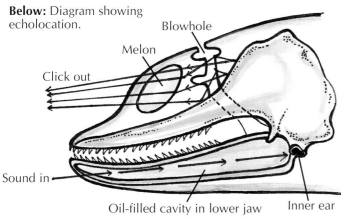

Blowhole

Melon

Click out

Sound in

Oil-filled cavity in lower jaw

Inner ear

Like the larger whales, dolphins have a natural sonar system known as echolocation. Sounds in the form of clicks leave the animal's body through the melon, fatty tissue located above the forehead. By listening to the echoes that bounce off objects, the dolphin can find fish and navigate its way among other animals.

LIFE CYCLE

Most species live at least twenty-five years, with bottlenose dolphins having a life span of thirty years. Sharks are their main natural enemy, and for this reason dolphins often swim in groups, taking turns to look out for predators. Other causes of death are stranding or getting caught in fishing nets.

For many dolphin species, there is no fixed breeding season. Like most whales, dolphins are very physical. Courtship rituals include males bumping heads with females, chasing them, and rubbing fins.

For most species, pregnancy takes ten to twelve months and there is usually only one baby or calf born at a time. Sometimes other females act as "midwives," helping the mother to give birth. The calf is pushed to the surface to take its first breath. Fathers take no part in caring for the young.

Dolphin herds range from tens to several thousand animals. They will often split up into smaller groups at night to feed, coming back together during the day to rest and play. Family groups usually consist of dominant males, several females and their young, and a few immature dolphins of both sexes. In some

Below: Competition between males for the attention of females results in biting, chasing and ramming. Mating scratches are commonly seen on dolphins.

26

Left: Hector's dolphin calves are thirty inches when born. Baby dolphins are looked after and nursed for about a year from the mother's special milk-producing glands.

Below: Maui, a lone bottlenose, spent many months around the coast of New Zealand interacting with people. Some dolphins form close-knit family groups, while others are solitary animals.

species the ties between animals are strong enough for them to help another dolphin in trouble. They will use their backs or flippers to keep an ill or injured dolphin near the surface so it can breathe.

Dolphins do not migrate on the same scale as baleen whales. Any movements they do make are likely to be the result of searching for food rather than moving to specific breeding grounds.

27

DOLPHIN TALK and INTELLIGENCE

Dolphins are noisy creatures, constantly sending out sounds such as clicks, whistles, squeaks, and barks. The clicks are short pulses of about three hundred sounds per second, used in echolocation. Whistles are used to communicate alarm, excitement, and other emotional states. For example, loud sounds accompanied by tail-slapping and clapping jaws together are thought to be a sign of anger. Whistles also seem to help identify a particular animal, with each dolphin having its own "tune."

Some researchers believe dolphins have their own kind of language. This is important in communicating

Below: The streams of fine bubbles coming from the dolphins' blowholes are visual signs of communication whistles.

with each other when they swim and hunt in groups. Much of the dolphin's large brain is taken up with processing this barrage of sounds.

It is thought that dolphins might be capable of learning a true language and communicating with people, and some animals have been taught to make the sounds of a few human words. Other signs of intelligence are their ability to learn and carry out difficult tasks in captivity. Many trainers give instructions in the form of arm and hand signals.

Dolphins have excellent memories and can copy behavior as well as invent their own games. The fact that they are also able to solve problems makes them more intelligent than any other group of animals, except for monkeys and apes.

DOLPHINS and PEOPLE

There is a long history of attraction between dolphins and people. Pictures of dolphins appear on the murals and pottery of ancient Greece and the animals appear in many stories in both Greek and Roman mythology. There are numerous stories of dolphins helping sailors, fishermen, and swimmers in distress but not one of a dolphin causing a person harm. The dolphin is the only animal that gives friendship for no advantage to themselves.

Unfortunately, they have not been well repaid for their friendliness and helpfulness. Dolphins used to be hunted commercially, particularly for the small quantities of valuable oil from parts of their head. In countries like Peru and Japan, thousands of dolphins are still

Above: A Pacific white-sided dolphin is trapped in a fishing net. Thousands of dolphins drown this way each year.

Right: The "Monkey Mia" bottlenose dolphins in Western Australia are world famous. Every day visitors play with and feed fish to the pod of about ten "wild" dolphins that venture into very shallow water.

Left: Swimming with dolphins has become a popular tourist activity. Some dolphins seem to enjoy close physical contact with humans.

killed each year for meat eaten by both people and animals. A number of porpoises, such as Dall's and the common or harbor porpoise, are also caught for food.

Many more dolphins become accidentally trapped in nets used to fish tuna. (Dolphins often swim with schools of tuna.) Between 1959 and 1972, an estimated 4.5 million dolphins died in this way. Consumer pressure has forced tuna canners to refuse to accept shipments from fishing fleets that do not protect dolphins. Some cans of tuna on supermarket shelves now carry a dolphin-friendly logo.

Populations of dolphins are also on the decline in certain parts of the industrialized world due to water pollution and the disappearance of their food base through overfishing.

INDEX

First published in 1997 by David Bateman Ltd.,
30 Tarndale Grove, Albany Business Park,
Albany, Auckland, New Zealand

Copyright © David Bateman Ltd., 1997

First edition for the United States and Canada
published by Barron's Educational Series, Inc., 1997

Text: Judith Hodge, B.A. (Hons)
Editorial consultant: Michael Donoghue, M.Sc.
Photographs: Malcolm Francis, Key-Light Image Library,
Natural Images, New Zealand Picture Library, Clive Roberts
(Museum of New Zealand), Sea Watch Foundation, Robert
Suisted, Kim Westerskov
Illustrations: Caren Glazer
Design: Errol McLeary

All inquiries should be addressed to:
Barron's Educational Series, Inc.
250 Wireless Boulevard
Hauppauge, New York 11788

Library of Congress Catalog Card No. 97-17312
International Standard Book No. 0-7641-0259-1

Library of Congress Cataloging-in-Publication Data
Hodge, Judith, 1963–
     Dolphins / Judith Hodge. —1st ed. for the U.S. and
Canada.
          p. cm. — (Animals of the oceans)
     Originally published: Auckland, N.Z. : D. Bateman
        Ltd., 1995.
     Includes index.
     Summary: Describes the physical characteristics,
behavior, life cycle, and different kinds of dolphins.
     ISBN 0-7641-0259-1
     1. Dolphins—Juvenile literature. [1. Dolphins.]
I. Title. II. Series.
QL737.C432H625 1997
599.53—dc21   97-17312
                                                     CIP
                                                      AC
Printed in China
9 8 7 6